ECK WISDOM
on
Soul Travel

ECK WISDOM

on

Soul Travel

HAROLD KLEMP

ECKANKAR
Minneapolis
www.Eckankar.org

ECK Wisdom on Soul Travel

Copyright © 2019 ECKANKAR

Printed in USA

Photo of Sri Harold Klemp (page 80)
by Art Galbraith

Library of Congress Cataloging-in-Publication Data

Names: Klemp, Harold, author.

Title: ECK wisdom on soul travel / Harold Klemp.

Description: Minneapolis : Eckankar, 2019.

Identifiers: LCCN 2019002962 | ISBN 9781570434778 (pbk. : alk. paper)

Subjects: LCSH: Eckankar (Organization)--Doctrines. | Soul--Eckankar (Organization) | Astral projection.

Classification: LCC BP605.E3 K553877 2019 | DDC 299/.93--dc23 LC record available at https://lccn.loc.gov/2019002962

∞ This paper meets the requirements of ANSI/NISO Z39.48-1992 (Permanence of Paper).

CONTENTS

OUT OF THE BODY

*Y*ears ago Julia, a college student, crammed two nights in a row to prepare for final exams. The third day she completed the last of them. Near exhaustion, she went straight home to rest, and seconds after her head hit the pillow, Julia was in slumberland.

But then something quite extraordinary occurred: she was suddenly out of her body.

There she stood, off to one side of the bed, studying her room. She also inspected her human body, an inert cloak on the bed. An odd thought came to mind: *Should I phone my mother to let her know?* Know what?

Did I die? she wondered. That would certainly be news and worth a call.

1

This was Julia's first out-of-the-body experience. She didn't know that a spiritual guide was on hand to protect her. Yet she did feel a definite mantle of love and protection around her.

Something away from the bed now caught her eye. Outside her bedroom window appeared a column of blazing blue-white light. It was six to eight feet around and filled her entire vision. There came a sound too. Much like a rushing wind, it nevertheless had more of a pulsing, electrical tone.

Then Julia awoke in bed again, fully united with her human body.

Many years would pass yet before she would actually meet the Master who introduced her to the Light and Sound of ECK on that day of final exams.

Julia's is one of many ways that the love of ECK, Divine Spirit, comes to those who wish it. Spiritual experiences, like those reported in the Bible, are alive and well, continuing since the days of yore. Nor have they existed only as the singular experiences of saints; unsung average people, like Julia, continue to have them too.

Soul Travel is just the beginning!

WHAT IS SOUL TRAVEL?

*T*o back up just a bit, what is Soul?

You are Soul, an eternal, individual spark of God. Soul is the True Self, the real you. One of a kind, on a divine journey back to the heart of God.

So, in the simplest terms, Soul Travel is an individual moving closer to the heart of God. Some people experience it as the apparent movement of the Soul body through the planes of time and space.*

Yet Soul exists on all planes, so what feels like movement, or travel, is simply Soul coming into an agreement with fixed

---

* The heavenly worlds contain many levels, or planes. Please see the chart on page 13 for an overview.

states and conditions that already exist in some world of time and space.

In Soul Travel you may experience a rushing sound, like wind in a tunnel, and the sensation of moving incredibly fast. But really, Soul doesn't move; Soul *is*. Time and space adjust to Soul's state of consciousness, and it is this adjustment of time and space that gives the impression of movement or speed.

Another form of Soul Travel is the expansion of consciousness.

This aspect is the true state of personal revelation or enlightenment that we aspire to in ECK. It visits both the timid and the bold, and is a gentler, less robust version of movement in consciousness. Most people experience this sort of gradual shifting of awareness.

In the broadest sense, Soul Travel can be used in every aspect of your daily life. It encompasses much more than merely traveling out of the body. It is the expansion of consciousness which allows you to get along every day with more awareness of the greater wisdom and understanding that is coming to you from the Holy Spirit.

Love and wonder define Soul Travel the best.

GOLDEN KISS OF GOD

*S*oul Travel is thus of several dimensions. Some people describe it as a shift in consciousness. Out of the blue, some event happens to shed light on a spiritual matter that had mystified them. A shift in consciousness to a new plane flits in like a soft, golden kiss of God. Then, these lucky Souls *know* they've had the best of good fortune and have touched the hem of divine love. Rather, it has brushed them.

Soul Travel, as stated, may also be of a more dramatic sort. In this case, an individual transcends the human body and tastes the love and freedom that are a birthright. He rises into the other worlds. Each experience fits him, because each is but a reflection of the individual's spiritual state.

People ask, "Why is it so important in Eckankar to learn Soul Travel?"

Soul Travel, in a broad sense, is of much value because it is a link to the expansion of consciousness. The rule of destiny holds that people at some time will begin to awaken to who and what they are. A knowledge of past lives may also open to them by way of dreams or déjà vu. A few catch a glimpse of future events.

With this higher state of consciousness comes a degree of perception, happiness, and a mental clarity beyond description. It is a state in which the individual feels natural, where the individual says, "This is what I am: I am Soul, I am eternal, and I would like to stay here forever."

Now having proof that there is life beyond the physical body, the person constantly strives to return to this higher state.

It's an exciting, interesting experience, and the way to bring it about is through the spiritual exercises. When ready for it, the student of ECK is given this experience in the other worlds of God, in the heavens which are spoken of in the many different religions. And once he has the actual experience, he comes back the knower. There is a world of difference between knowing and believing.

Belle's Soul Travel Experience

Belle was satisfied with her life. Her dream life was active, and she could recognize the Holy Spirit (ECK) at work in her daily life. And most of all, she was seeing the Light and hearing the Sound of God. Yet she recognized a complacency in herself; maybe she did need to learn Soul Travel.

Belle became like a fresh student, starting all over, working step-by-step with the spiritual exercises. She disciplined herself to wake up in the middle of the night to record any dream impressions. Like a child always keeping her parent in sight, she looked for Spirit in everything.

At this point, Belle realized she wanted God-Realization more than anything else in the world. Then came the Soul Travel experience. It was tailor-made exactly for her.

Belle awoke in bed, hearing her husband talking loudly in the hall and bumping the bathroom door with his foot. It annoyed her. Then with a start, she noticed he was also lying in bed beside her. Her first reaction was panic. All that moved were her eyes, gazing back and forth from the hall to the bed. Calming down, she thought, *After all, he's out of his body; I'm not out of mine.* But her guide, the Mahanta, the Inner Master, was gradually preparing her for what was really happening.

Next Belle felt herself floating upward into another dimension. It was like turning up a dimmer switch in a darkened room; it revealed the scene of an old general store. In her waking life, she had a weakness for exploring every old general store that came along.

This store was clean and bright. Belle's two young daughters, dressed in old-fashioned attire, were sitting on barstools, eating ice cream. The Mahanta spoke softly to her, "Look around." Still timid, she turned her head slowly. It was comforting to see the Master and her two daughters in the store, but she also needed the comfort of her physical body and the presence of her husband beside her in bed. So she was able to go back and forth between her bed and the Astral Plane, where this Soul Travel experience had taken her.

Again the Master said, "Look around." *Now this is real freedom*, she thought. Then, ever so gently, Belle floated back to her body, retaining the love and joy of the experience.

Whispering her thanks to the Mahanta, it occurred to her that he had been kind enough to start her with an old general store, which keenly interested her.

Then it struck her: Soul Travel has a lot to do with getting interested in things, starting with the physical world. This gives the ECK more to work with. And if one is truly interested in something, how can there be any room for fear?

THE WORLDS OF ECK

(Plane)	(Chant)	(Sound)
ANAMI LOK	HU (HYOO)	HU
AGAM LOK	HUK (HOOK)	MUSIC OF WOODWINDS
HUKIKAT LOK	ALUK (ah-LOOK)	THOUSAND VIOLINS
ALAYA LOK	HUM (HYOOM)	HUMMING SOUND
ALAKH LOK	SHANTI (SHAHN-tee)	WIND
ATMA LOK (Soul Plane)	SUGMAD (SOOG-mahd)	SINGLE NOTE OF A FLUTE

HIGHER WORLDS — Positive (left margin)

GOD-REALIZATION (right margin)

ETHERIC (Intuition)   BAJU (BAH joo)   BUZZING BEES
The last barrier between the lower worlds and the pure positive God Worlds.

- -

MENTAL (Mind)   AUM (AHM or ah UHM)   RUNNING WATER
Source of all mental teachings, aesthetics, philosophies, conventional concepts of God, cosmic consciousness.

CAUSAL (Memory)   MANA (MAH-nah)   TINKLING BELLS
Plane where memories, karmic patterns, and Akashic records are stored. The Causal body is also the seed body. Plane of negative reality, which affects all below.

ASTRAL (Emotion)   KALA (kah-LAH)   ROAR OF THE SEA
Source of all psychic phenomena—ghosts, flying saucers, spirits, ESP. Plane reached by astral projection and most occult sciences.

PHYSICAL (Senses)   ALAYI (ah-LAH-yee)   THUNDER
Plane where Soul is trapped by the five passions: lust, anger, greed, vanity, and attachment. Plane of time, space, and matter. Illusion of reality.

LOWER WORLDS — Negative (left margin)

SELF-REALIZATION (right margin)

13

In My Experience

The Spiritual Exercises of ECK lead to Self-Realization and God-Realization, and from this come the attributes of wisdom, charity, and freedom.

These spiritual exercises link you with the guidance of the Holy Spirit, which is seen as Light and heard as Sound. The inner Sound is the Voice of God calling you home. The inner Light is a beacon to light your way. All the Spiritual Exercises of ECK are built on these two divine aspects of the Holy Spirit.

Learning spiritual consciousness is learning how to live in this world no matter what comes. You learn through these spiritual exercises how to live life graciously, from childhood to old age. You learn how to live life in the best way possible.

The Spiritual Exercises of ECK give you confidence in yourself. You learn that you are Soul, you are eternal. Then you know with certainty that you live forever, that death cannot destroy you.

You can do the spiritual exercises in a number of different ways. Usually, any guidelines I give are to help you develop the self-discipline to remember what's happening on the inner planes.

When I first began practicing the spiritual exercises, I was scared. I tried some of the positions that Paul Twitchell, the modern-day founder of Eckankar, mentioned—sitting on the floor tailor-fashion, legs crossed, back erect. I started by sitting in the middle of the floor, but as soon as I began to put attention on my contemplation, my body slumped—and that would jolt me out of the experience.

15

The next level of experimentation in my evolution with these exercises was to sit with my back against a wall. This resulted in a 25 percent improvement: Now I could only fall sideways or forward.

When I found a comfortable position, I could relax, shut my eyes, and look at the inner screen. It was like watching a movie screen. Sometimes it was black, sometimes white, sometimes gray. There were even times when I could actually see a scene or a moving picture.

For a while I looked straight into it. Sometimes that worked, but eventually it didn't. Occasionally I let my inner vision stray to the left about ten degrees or so, and then suddenly I would notice that something had appeared on the screen. This is how I began to look for the Master. In a relaxed way I would look to the side, knowing that my attention was really toward the center. And then I would start to chant *HU*, the ancient name for God, or another sacred word.

These were some of the things I tried, but the greatest obstacle that held me back at the time was fear. Even while I was trying to go out of the body, I was afraid I might really do it!

Paul always recommended that we do the spiritual exercises sitting up, but necessity forced me into different positions. While in the service, I certainly wasn't about to sit on the floor with my legs crossed, hands folded, and eyes shut. In the barracks the cubicles were an open area and there were always a lot of other airmen around. I was with the security service; we had a top-secret classification, and they are very selective of the people who come in there. They like to be sure you're stable. If they see you sitting on the floor doing strange things, it won't be long before you'll find yourself in some other line of work—

without your top-secret clearance. I had a good job, and I wanted to keep it; so I figured if I did the spiritual exercises sitting up, I was dumber than I looked. That's when I started doing them while lying down in bed.

Out-of-the-Body Experience

One of my early out-of-body experiences happened when I was stationed with the National Security Agency at Fort Meade, Maryland. One Saturday night about ten o'clock, after everyone else had left the barracks, I lay down on the bed, pulled up the covers, and stretched out as straight and stiff as a mummy. This position had occasionally brought comments from my friends, such as, "You sure sleep strange." Later I learned how to do the spiritual exercises lying on my side, so I didn't look quite so obvious. But at the time, the move from the floor to the bed was a big jump in my spiritual evolution.

18

While lying there with my eyes closed, doing a spiritual exercise, I began to hear a whirring sound that grew increasingly louder. All of a sudden it felt like I was floating. Not yet realizing I was in the Soul body running the astral form, I thought maybe I was levitating.

It's not like a dream when these things happen—you're right there.

As I started rising higher, I wondered if I really might be floating, so I opened my eyes—and was startled to find myself above the pillow. *This is really neat*, I thought. The next thing, I'm settling back down on the bed. I noticed that as I began to go down, the whirring sound subsided. There seemed to be a relationship between my elevation and the intensity and pitch of the sound. The lower it got, the lower I went. "No, no, no!" I said. "Up! Up! Up!" But I went down, down, down. *Rats!* I thought. Out of the body and I couldn't stay there. I blew it.

When my body settled back down I decided to get out of bed, but it was very difficult to move. I couldn't understand why. It felt like somebody was holding me down. It took all my strength to get to the edge of the bed. Finally I rolled out, hit the floor, and came bouncing up. I thought, *Boy, that was some experience. I'd better write it down before I forget it.* I didn't yet realize I wasn't back in the body.

I looked around then and saw that the sheets on the bed had spilled out onto the floor. But my perceptions had changed. The vision I had at that point was different than I was used to. My seeing power was like tunnel vision. Anything I gazed at, I could see, and the only thing I cared about was what I gazed at. It commanded my complete attention.

It was when I picked up the sheets that I noticed this pulsing bluish thing that gave off a luminous glow. It was the silver cord, the line which holds the material bodies to the various planes. But it looked more like a bluish-white plastic hose. It was actually pulsing with life. The strange thing was, I couldn't tell where this silver cord was attached. I knew it was connected to me somewhere—but where?

As I studied it intently and tried to figure it out, I happened to look over at the bed, and that's when I saw myself lying there. I wasn't impressed at all. One's sleeping body, especially when viewed unexpectedly, isn't exactly the greatest thing in the world to see. In sleep everything shows.

Proof of Soul's Survival

It felt great to be out of the body, but I wasn't sure what to do next. I'd picked up the sheets—done my housekeeping—but now what? You know the saying about how the devil finds work for idle hands. It was that kind of thing, but mostly it was the desire to explore, to try something new, to have an adventure.

I glanced around and saw the television set in the next cubicle, a makeshift room comprised of lockers that were arranged in a semibarrier. But this TV was brown, whereas on the Physical Plane it was white.

If you walk around your home in the inner worlds, you'll find it's a little bit different. The television set might be another color or another size; your house might be bigger or smaller. Don't fight it—it's just a different world than our creation down here. The Physical Plane builders fashioned your house here because there was already an image of it on the Astral Plane, and they got as close as they could. So the TV set may end up white here instead of brown.

Just as I was trying to figure out my next move, I heard somebody walking up the center aisle that separated the cubicles that lined each side of the barracks. The footsteps sounded like he was approaching very quickly. I thought it was one of my roommates and tried to face him, but I couldn't get turned around. The glowing cord seemed to hinder my movements in certain directions. Maybe I was tangled up in it. It occurred to me that if I backed up so that I stood in his path, he would have to walk right through a ghost. Wouldn't that be a laugh! Would he feel a cold wind? I was experimenting and having a good time.

All of a sudden a man comes walking right up to me. I was standing in the middle of the aisle, but there was enough space behind me for him to slip into my cubicle. Later, after seeing his picture on a book cover, I learned it was Paul Twitchell, but at the time I took him for an intruder.

When the stranger walked over and stood in a dark corner by the dresser, my happy mood suddenly changed to fear. *I'm out of my body*, I thought. *What am I going to do if he hurts it?*

There I was in a world that was so much

lighter and better, and I found myself worrying about the thing I had been making fun of just a few minutes ago.

The fellow stayed over in the corner, leaning against the dresser, one ankle crossed over the other. All he did was stand there, calmly observing me. But fear has an interesting effect.

I rushed at him. "No! Don't go near my body!" He wasn't making a move toward it. "Go away!" I shouted, waving my arms the way you'd shoo a goose. "Go away!"

The next thing I knew, I was lying on the bed. There had been no sense of transition at all. At first I couldn't figure out where I was, but I finally realized I was back in the physical body. When I rolled out of bed this time, my body moved quickly. I glanced toward the dresser—nobody was there.

What this experience taught me was that whoever I am, I am me. My Real Self had nothing to do with the physical body or even a body running around on the Astral Plane. This was my proof of the survival of Soul, a greater consciousness that lived outside of and beyond the Physical or the Astral body.

LEARNING TO SOUL TRAVEL

*B*eginners in Soul Travel like to stay close to the body. It gives them confidence. So the Mahanta or another ECK Master will help them shed the human state of consciousness and stick to a short journey into a higher plane.

"Ann" lived in an apartment. She had learned to Soul Travel in her dreams but often wondered why she never traveled beyond her apartment building.

Each time Ann fell asleep and awoke in the Soul body, she could see her physical body lying on the bed. Her routine was to walk through her front door and out into the hallway of the building. There she'd wait. By and by, the Inner Master would appear from around the corner.

"Where do you want to go?" he'd say.

Her usual answer was, "I want to go to a Golden Wisdom Temple." Yet the apartment building was the extent of her Soul Travel journeys.

One night she asked the Inner Master why she never left her living quarters in her dreams. "Please show me what I need to do."

"How did you learn to Soul Travel?" he asked.

So she began thinking about the first time she had found herself out of the body.

Finding Yourself Out of the Body

During that initial experience with Soul Travel, Ann had walked into the kitchen and the bedroom to look around her apartment.

"Hey, this is great," she'd said.

Each step of the way she'd thought of

what to do next. It took her a while in the dream state to think of chanting "Wah Z," the spiritual name of the Inner Master. This name took her to a higher level. Though her intuition urged some new experiment, nothing at first came to mind. But then it occurred to her to sit on the couch and do a spiritual exercise in her dream.

The spiritual exercise took her out of her apartment, into the hallway. There she had met the Inner Master.

That was the first and last experiment she had ever tried.

Finally, Ann understood why the Master didn't come up to her in the dream state and say, "OK, we'll go off to a Wisdom Temple. I'll do everything for you; you don't have to do anything."

The Dream Master wanted her to use her own creativity and initiative.

Most often, someone fails at Soul Travel or dream travel because of a fear of death.

Ann started to experiment and have the experience of Soul Travel under her own terms, so this fear began to vanish.

Answer to a Prayer

Soul Travel is a very enriching part of Eckankar. Its main benefit is to let us tap into the wisdom and knowledge we've gained in the other worlds. Thus we may enjoy a heightened state of awareness twenty-four hours a day.

It is in this way that the inner and outer experiences build upon each other, to bring more love, joy, and understanding into our lives. This deep insight into the workings of everyday life is more important than any single experience out of the body.

However, Soul Travel incorporates many experiences from the inner worlds and weaves them into a tapestry of exquisite beauty and value beyond price.

That is Soul Travel.

"Betty" was a mother, very close to her son; she found Eckankar after his death in a motorcycle mishap. Devastated by the loss, she was unable to find comfort in church. She would cry through the whole service. If she could but feel closer to God, then maybe He would help her understand why the accident had occurred.

More important, where was her son now? Was he OK?

Her prayers for help in understanding were endless.

Five months later, while at her lowest ebb, there came an experience that changed her life. She thought first it was a dream, but it was in fact Soul Travel.

Betty awoke in vivid consciousness in the other worlds. A bespectacled woman with gray streaks in her dark hair met Betty, and they talked for a few minutes.

"Do you know my son?" Betty asked, giving his name.

"Of course I know him," said the other. "He lives right over there in that white house." The scene, a pastoral setting of cottages, looked like a lake resort.

There she found her son, and they had a long conversation. He assured her that his health was better than it had been on earth. Then he looked at her and said, "I know what you're doing to yourself. Please stop. You're hurting yourself."

Before they parted, she asked if she could hold him in her arms, since she didn't get a chance to do so before his death. Merry laughter twinkled in his eyes.

"OK, Mom," he said.

Soul Travel had brought her to him. She could still feel his warmth in her arms when she awoke. Even his scent lingered. A peaceful, happy feeling lasted for weeks before it began to fade. Betty became determined to learn all about her son's new home in heaven. Somewhere on earth, she knew, someone had the answer. That was the juncture where her sister introduced her to Eckankar.

The first book Betty read was *The Spiritual Notebook*, by Paul Twitchell. It convinced her that here was the answer to her prayers. Here was an explanation about the other worlds that made sense.

Grief for her son still overtakes Betty on occasion. So she looks to the Mahanta, the Living ECK Master to help her regain the tranquillity she felt while with her son during Soul Travel. She continues to do the Spiritual Exercises of ECK every day.

Betty now directs her efforts toward seeing the divine Light and hearing the holy Sound—keys to the secret worlds of God.

Beyond its exciting side, Soul Travel is a direct way to hear the Sound and see the Light of God. That cannot be done from the human consciousness. The Sound and Light are the wave of divine love that Soul catches into the kingdom of heaven; they are the twin aspects of the ECK, the Holy Spirit.

The ECK is the Voice of God, the Comforter, the spirit of truth.

By the time one learns the secrets of visions, dreams, Soul Travel, and Self-Realization, he is an experienced traveler in the high regions of God.

Then comes the crown of realization, the enlightenment of God.

Experience is our hallmark in ECK. An individual may read all the books on faith and spirituality in a metropolitan library, but reading nets him nothing in the God Worlds. Only experience goes beyond the detours and dead ends of life. Only experience reveals the correct road to the realm of the All.

So a milestone in Soul's supreme journey to God is the art and science of Soul Travel.

A Gateway to Soul Travel

*I*f you want to learn Soul Travel, do this technique tonight. Before sleep, shut your eyes and place your attention on the Spiritual Eye. It's right above and between the eyebrows.

Then sing *HU*, an ancient, sacred name of God. Fill your heart, mind, and body with warm love.

This feeling of love grants the confidence to venture into some new, unexplored area of your spiritual being. A way to fill yourself with love is to call up a warm, comfy memory, like a child's hug or a mate's kiss.

Just so the feeling warms your heart with deep love.

Now, eyes still shut, look into the Spiritual Eye for the holy person who is your ideal, whether Christ or an ECK Master. In a gentle voice say, "I give you permission to take me to the best place for my spiritual good."

Then chant *HU*, *God*, or some other holy word.

Next, see yourself in a familiar place, like a special room in your home. Be assured that the guide who comes is a dear, long-standing friend.

Do this session five or six times over as many days.

A spiritual exercise is like a physical exercise in that all muscles need time to respond. So do this spiritual exercise at least a week before you consider throwing in the towel. Success comes with diligence. And if you do this exercise for a couple of weeks, you may surprise yourself at your new spiritual outlook.

A RARE, DIFFERENT SORT OF SOUL TRAVEL

*N*ow let's look at a striking, but rare sort of Soul Travel. It shows how this ancient science blends into the affairs and circumstances of each seeker's makeup.

"Michael," from Ghana, once had an experience that shook his beliefs about physical reality. The experience raised some questions. Those concerns led him, in the several years to come, on a search for answers.

Michael has a practical mind, albeit a very complex one. So an ECK Master sent him on a unique out-of-body trip to challenge and expand his understanding.

Michael had heard and read about people in Ghana, non-ECKists, who'd become lost in strange, invisible, and mysterious towns that they claimed did not exist. Their experiences confounded them. After they told their tales, it was next to impossible to believe them. Moreover, there were also stories of people who'd died but were reported in encounters in other parts of Ghana. Sometimes these "dead" people vanished into thin air when a living person confronted them.

But none of that was on Michael's mind on that ordinary day as he set out on some personal errands in the city of Accra.

A taxi dropped him off at his first stop without incident. His business in the government office lasted ten minutes. The next stop was a short distance away, along a tree-shaded street, so Michael decided to walk. From there, errands done, he took a fancy to walk home.

That is where he entered a twilight zone.

A tall, stout man of thirty-five called to him from behind. "Do you know the location of the Ministry of Education Annex?"

Michael said no. They parted ways.

Five minutes later Michael was lost. He thought he knew the streets of Accra like the back of his hand, but the unfamiliar streets and buildings around him were a labyrinth of confusion. What was going on? Michael asked directions. He followed one through a narrow lane set between a house and a mansion.

His position was hopeless. What part of Accra could this be?

The experience ran on, taking him outside the city to a suburb. But that town lay in the wrong direction. Petrol (service) stations, churches, the city's traffic circle—all familiar locations—were either gone or changed in appearance.

Poor Michael. To say he was in a confused state is to make light of his misfortune.

Nor could he retrace his steps. Streets were new or laid out in a different way. Worse, the service station of a few minutes ago had vanished, as had a beer bar with a blue canopy over the door. Michael only broke free of this experience after he caught a regular city bus from that suburb to Accra.

Later, he could not duplicate the route of his strange journey into an even stranger dimension.

Of course, it perplexed him.

He'd never read of anything like it in the ECK teachings, but he drew a few conclusions on his own. First, was it possible that this physical plane had many levels that are kept separate from each other by different vibrations? Can such exist side by side, invisible to each other?

Yes, it's true. No absolute line of demarcation separates the Physical Plane from the

Astral Plane, so the very top vibrations of the physical world blend into the lower astral region beyond.

Then crossover visits occur.

Second, the question, When did he enter the invisible world?

He concluded that it all began when the tall, stout stranger called to him from behind. (That stranger was an ECK Master. He'd come to help Michael expand his state of consciousness in a manner that fit Michael's state of awareness.)

To sum up, this otherworldly experience began with the stranger and ended with Michael on a bus back to familiar grounds in Accra.

Of interest here is that Michael could not escape this strange morass of events without the impartial aid of a bus driver. To be sure, this was an uncommon Soul Travel experience. Yet it taught Michael that the stories he'd heard about strange towns and people in Ghana were true. A Westerner might have a good laugh at such a tale, but the people of Ghana know better.

And so does Michael.

REALITY ON
THE INNER PLANES

*W*hen I go into the other worlds, I am there; it's not a dream. Many of the higher ECK initiates also spend time in the other worlds, moving about and doing things. I don't have the words to describe it; the best I can do is show you how to get there and find out for yourself.

The description of heaven given by the orthodox religions is a relic left over from the early days of Christianity. It is a heaven that has stopped evolving—an anachronism, lost in time. The heavens we find today are not as described in the Bible. Rather than wearing long robes, the people you meet in heaven these days are dressed similarly to those you meet here in the physical plane.

At times you may be taken to a paradise. You might have some revelation or illumination during these isolated instances of Soul Travel, but then you have to come back here to earth and learn how to deal with it.

On the inner planes you are also running a body similar to the one you have here. You are not just dealing with people on one plane; you are interacting on many planes, on many different levels.

By operating in the Soul body, one is able to draw experiences from a number of different bodies, or vehicles, at the same time. Some people use only one or two, but others run a number of different bodies, not only here on earth but also in the other planes.

Soul Travel is simply Soul's movement to God.

This practice is what many devotees of

world religions have sought in vain in their own teachings. Soul Travel is an active method of going home to God. The term itself is a dynamic way to express this natural means of ascending to the pinnacle of heaven or plumbing the depths of God's love for Its creation.

Soul Travel is also a cleansing agent for Soul.

Rather than expect you to grasp a full understanding of the philosophy behind Soul Travel, I give stories and examples to tell of its workings. In time, with your own experience as a gauge, you will know what's most important here. The words on these pages are like flower seeds planted in the fertile soil of your heart. You'll remember all you need to, when you need to, for taking a new step toward the infinite love and mercy of God.

Everything has a time and season. So be patient.

SPIRITUAL EXERCISES
FOR SOUL TRAVEL

*W*hen you step onto the path to God and you begin looking for that secret path to heaven, the way will be opened for you. And the way lies through the Spiritual Exercises of ECK.

These spiritual exercises promote Soul Travel—the movement of the inner consciousness.

Here are four exercises for you to try.

First Landmarks of Soul Travel

One way to leave the body via Soul Travel is to lie down after dinner when you are drowsy. Plan to nap for five minutes,

45

and watch the process of falling asleep. If you try the exercise with your spouse, agree to meet outside the body a few minutes later. Then watch carefully as your mate steps free of the physical body and enters the spiritual one in a burst of radiant light.

One always goes out of the body when he falls asleep, but it is an unconscious act. In Soul Travel, the only difference is that we are trying to get out of the body in full awareness.

The moment Soul leaves the body, It finds Itself in a blue-gray zone near the Physical Plane. This zone is an approach to the Astral Plane. The sensation of moving from the Physical to the Astral body is like slipping through a large iris of mild wind currents; this iris is the Spiritual Eye. Soul enters this neutral zone of blue-gray tones in Its astral form, a sheath which looks like a thousand sparkling stars.

This buffer zone, or corridor, between

the Physical and lower Astral Planes resembles the underground silo of an enormous rocket that is perhaps two hundred feet in diameter and more than two thousand feet deep. The ceiling of this circular pocket is open and may display a brilliant canopy of white light, or you may see a night sky sprinkled with specks of twinkling stars. There may even be a pastoral scene by a river, whose waters murmur their pleasure at life.

Whatever scene is displayed in the opening of the vast ceiling, Soul is drawn toward it at a mighty speed. Most people begin to recall their dreams only after their departure from this launching zone between the two worlds, and after their arrival at a faraway destination on the Astral Plane.

Around the Room

This spiritual exercise uses the imaginative body. Take a seat in a chair. Make yourself comfortable. Then say, "I shall go for a short walk in the Soul body." Close your eyes, and look into the Spiritual Eye in a soft, sweet, gentle way. Sing *HU* for a minute or two, and then imagine yourself getting up.

If I were doing this contemplation, I would say, "I will get out of the chair in the Soul body and walk in front of the table. I will become very interested in the things around me, such as the color of the tablecloth, the flowers, and the vase.

"While the physical body is still in contemplation with its eyes shut, I will walk in the imaginative body to look at the curtains. I will touch the curtains and notice how nice this beautiful yellow cloth feels."

Become curious, and decide to see what's beneath the curtain. Observe the floor beneath the curtain, and pay very close attention to every little detail.

Now go over to the door, and turn the

knob. Notice what the doorknob looks like. Before you open the door, say, "On the other side I'm going to see the Inner Master." Then open the door. Sure enough, he's there, and he says, "Are you ready to go yet? Let's take a walk outside."

The Imaginative Technique

With the imaginative technique for Soul Travel, you imagine a scene, and you are there in the Soul body. It may feel as though you are moving along very quickly, and this is why it is perceived as travel. Actually, it is the process of changing the setting around you.

To practice this, you can take a scene from your memories and control the actions in it. For example, imagine the sea beating against a beach. Now try to see the sea as being as still as lake water. Try it on things you know by stilling or stopping actions.

You may experience a rushing sound, like wind in a tunnel, and the sensation of moving incredibly fast.

A Spiritual Exercise for While You Sleep

If you wish to Soul Travel while you are asleep, remind yourself of this several times during the day. For example, say to yourself, "Tonight I will Soul Travel in my dream." Your mind will accept ideas that are repeated more readily than ideas that are not repeated.

Visualize the kind of dream you want to have as though it were already happening. After you have pictured the dream, picture its results. Try playing a movie scene in your mind of how you will feel when you have the advice or help you seek from the Dream Master.

QUESTIONS AND ANSWERS

$\mathcal{A}$s spiritual leader of Eckankar, I receive thousands of letters from seekers of truth around the world. All want direct and useful answers about how to travel the road to God. Here are several questions I've been asked relating to Soul Travel.

Purpose of Soul Travel

What's the purpose of Soul Travel? Is it more important than learning divine love, for example?

I am really more interested in having an individual open up to divine love than to achieve anything else, including Soul Travel. Soul Travel is the natural way for expansion of consciousness and travel into

51

the spiritual worlds of God. Yet all that it is, is one means available for you to find the love of God.

The path of ECK is much broader than Soul Travel, of course. There are many ways that Divine Spirit, the ECK, expresses Itself to the human race, but many of the ways seem so commonplace that the average person doesn't see or hear them anymore.

This includes all the sounds of nature: the sound of a gentle breeze, rustling leaves in autumn, the chirping of crickets, the purring of a cat, the low hum of a refrigerator, the laughing of children at play, and hundreds of other examples.

You mentioned your practice of former times where you went off by yourself to commune with God and nature. If you could ever recapture that, you would find much of the spiritual unfoldment you are looking for.

Our society admires more mental things

today: food for thought—either in writings or speeches. From this material, the Living ECK Master looks for an avenue to Soul that will result in the human mind stepping aside for a moment, letting the miracle of divine illumination occur.

You do not have to Soul Travel to be successful in ECK. Another way to God-Realization is to give tender love and care to every action, because of your love for God.

A direct and simple way to God is to find someone or something to love every day. Then, at bedtime, let your thoughts gently drift back to this moment of love in your day. Contemplate on that with love and joy. Your contemplative exercises can be as simple as that.

Do Animals Soul Travel?

I would like to know if animals such as lions, cows, and dogs have Soul Travel experiences.

Some animals do. They're the same as people, in that animals have many different levels of consciousness.

Like us, all animals dream. Some remember, many don't. Specially gifted ones, like spiritually advanced people, do Soul Travel. In time, scientific research will be able to expand its knowledge of what happens when people and animals sleep.

You can begin exploring your interests in these fields of knowledge through dreams or Soul Travel. Eventually, science will catch up to the knowledge of those who already can explore the spiritual states of living beings—human or animal—by Soul Travel.

When You Pass On

I would like to learn to Soul Travel in order to be prepared when I die. I am a little afraid of it now and would like it to be a joyful expe-

rience, since I am quite old and may be passing soon.

The ECK works in Its own way with each of us. It will bring whatever is right for our spiritual progress.

Some initiates never have Soul Traveled nor seen a particular manifestation of Divine Spirit, such as the Blue Light. We are all different.

It is of singular importance for us to contact the Mahanta, the Inner Master. Depending upon our station in life, we may become aware of either Light, Sound, or the appearance of the Inner Master. These are inward expressions.

Other valid signs of the ECK reported by initiates include a knowingness of divine intervention during the waking life. Otherwise it can be an impression of help from a mysterious source that one immediately accepts as the Holy Spirit.

It is not good if someone has too many

striking inner experiences, because all they may do is put the person out of step with friends and family. The secret of ECK is to live in step with all of life if that is possible.

The moment of passing from this life, or what is called translation, can be a wonderful experience, the highlight of Soul's chapter on earth. There is nothing special that one on the path of ECK has to do to prepare outwardly for the event. Make the usual arrangements for the disposal of the physical remains. Leave it in the hands of Divine Spirit to decide when the body is no longer suitable as a house for Soul.

I will be with you at the moment chosen for this occasion. This is usually a pleasant and spiritually invigorating event in one's life. As one enters into it, there come the memories of having done it before. All fear and doubt vanish. The radiant form of the Mahanta appears and takes the individual to the worlds of light and love.

What about Physical Limitations?

I have been partially paralyzed for much of my adult life. I read in one of the ECK books that no man with a defective body can ever become a spiritual traveler. This has really confused me, since I always felt that I would overcome this.

I got your question about whether certain people can qualify as candidates for spiritual travelers despite physical conditions.

Soul is not bound by any physical limitations.

The works of ECK bring out the eternal truths from a number of different approaches. One can choose that which fits him.

Some people are turned aside by what they consider to be incorrect grammar used by the ECK Masters, not realizing that the true spiritual foundation is set in the Light and Sound of God. At times the understanding of the human consciousness is not able to mentally comprehend the Master's words. All that's left then is to trust in the heart, and take our questions to the inner temple.

There is no spiritual limitation unless we ourselves allow it.

Experiencing Soul Travel

Sometimes when I am falling asleep, I feel like I am being lifted upward or moving around in a circle. What is that about?

The feeling of being lifted upward or moving around in a circle is one form of Soul Travel. Some of you had experiences like this as children, or even as adults. During the Spiritual Exercises of ECK you sometimes feel as if you're rising straight up, but it is not the physical body that's moving. You are being lifted upward in one of your inner bodies, either the Astral, Causal, Mental, or

Etheric body. Though you feel a physical sensation, you are being raised up spiritually.

This is one way Soul Travel works. More often it comes as a gradual shift in consciousness. When you lie down and go into contemplation during your spiritual exercises, all of a sudden you may find yourself in another setting, either on the Astral Plane, the Causal Plane, or the Mental Plane.

Suddenly you are there. You see other people, speak with them, and gain information and experience. When it's over, you are instantly back in the physical body, with no discomfort.

Can you imagine a child asking this question of a parent who knows nothing about Eckankar? These children were never told about the esoteric teachings of ECK, yet they are experiencing them.

But if the parents don't know what's

happening, what can they say? Their answer probably would be "It's a nightmare" or "It's only your imagination." Pretty soon the child shuts down this level of experience. After all, how could this be a valid part of human experience if no one has anything to say about it?

So when I write to these children, I recognize my responsibility to answer them in such a way that their parents can learn too.

How Do You Use Your Imagination?

I've heard that we should use our imagination to Soul Travel, but can we use too much imagination? Sometimes I'll have an experience and am not sure whether I've made it up.

To imagine Soul Travel is the first thing one must do before actually getting out of the body.

A girl who plays second base for a baseball team in town is called a "natural." But she works hard at her fielding and hitting. Her brothers are all good ballplayers, and in her mind she imagines herself every bit as good as they are. And so she *is* good, not only because of her imagination, but mainly because she practices harder than the other girls on the team.

Keep on imagining that you do Soul Travel, and one day you will suddenly do it. You will have no more doubt about the difference between imagination and Soul Travel.

Wait and see!

Next Steps in Spiritual Exploration

- **Try a spiritual exercise.**
  Review the spiritual exercises in this book or on our website.
  Experiment with them.

- **Browse our website: www.Eckankar.org.**
  Watch videos; get free books, answers to FAQs, and more info.

- **Attend a spiritual event in your area.**
  Visit "Eckankar around the World" on our website.

- **Begin your journey** with the Eckankar spiritual self-discovery courses that come with membership.

- **Read additional books** about the ECK teachings.

- **Call or write to us:** Call 1-800-LOVE GOD (1-800-568-3463, toll-free, automated) or (952) 380-2200 (direct).

- Write to: ECKANKAR, Dept. BK134, PO Box 2000, Chanhassen, MN 55317-2000 USA.

FOR FURTHER READING
By Harold Klemp

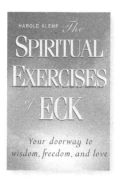

The Spiritual Exercises of ECK

This book is a staircase with 131 steps leading to the doorway to spiritual freedom, self-mastery, wisdom, and love. A comprehensive volume of spiritual exercises for every need.

ECK Wisdom on Conquering Fear

Would having more courage and confidence help you make the most of this lifetime?

Going far beyond typical self-help advice, this book invites you to explore divine love as the antidote to anxiety and the doorway to inner freedom.

You will discover ways to identify the karmic roots

63

of fear and align with your highest ideals.

Use this book to soar beyond your limitations and reap the benefits of self-mastery.

Live life to its fullest potential!

ECK Wisdom on Dreams

This dream study will help you be more *awake* than you've ever been!

ECK Wisdom on Dreams reveals the most ancient of dream teachings for a richer and more productive life today.

In this dynamic book, author Harold Klemp shows you how to remember your dreams, apply dream wisdom to everyday situations, recognize prophetic dreams, and more.

You will be introduced to the art of dream interpretation and offered techniques to discover the treasures of your inner worlds.

ECK Wisdom on Inner Guidance

Looking for answers, guidance, protection?

Help can come as a nudge, a dream, a vision, or a quiet voice within you. This book offers new ways to connect with the ever-present guidance of ECK, the Holy Spirit. Start today!

Discover how to listen to the Voice of God; attune to your true self; work with an inner guide; benefit from dreams, waking dreams, and Golden-tongued Wisdom; and ignite your creativity to solve problems.

Each story, technique, and spiritual exercise is a doorway to greater confidence and love for life.

Open your heart, and let God's voice speak to you!

ECK Wisdom on Karma and Reincarnation

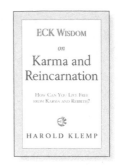

Have you lived before? What is the real meaning of life?

Discover your divine destiny—to move beyond the limits of karma and reincarnation and gain spiritual freedom.

This book reveals the purpose of living and the keys to spiritual growth.

You'll find answers to age-old questions about fate, destiny, and free will. These gems of wisdom can enhance your relationships, health, and happiness—and offer the chance to resolve all your karma in this lifetime!

ECK Wisdom on Life after Death

All that lies ahead is already within your heart.

ECK Wisdom on Life after Death invites you to explore the eternal nature of *you*!

Author Harold Klemp offers you new perspectives

on seeing heaven before you die, meeting with departed loved ones, near-death experiences, getting help from spiritual guides, animals in heaven, and dealing with grief.

Try the techniques and spiritual exercise included in this book to find answers and explore the secrets of life after death—for yourself.

ECK Wisdom on Solving Problems

Problems? Problems! Why do we have so many? What causes them? Can we avoid them?

Author Harold Klemp, the spiritual leader of Eckankar, can help you answer these questions and more. His sense of humor and practical approach offer spiritual keys to unlock the secrets to effective problem solving. Learn creative, time-tested techniques to

- Find the root cause of a problem
- Change your viewpoint and overcome difficulties
- Conquer your fears
- Work beyond symptoms to solutions

- Kindle your creativity
- Master your karma, past and present
- Receive spiritual guidance that can transform the way you see yourself and your life

ECK Wisdom on Spiritual Freedom

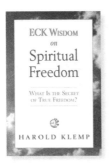

Are you everything you want to be? You came into this life to spread your wings and live in freedom—heart, mind, and Soul!

Author Harold Klemp puts the tools of spiritual freedom firmly in your grasp:

- Keys to embrace the highest expression of who you really are
- Techniques to tap into the divine Life Force for unlimited creativity and problem solving
- New paradigms to reveal the power of loving yourself, God, and all of life

What would you give for the secret of true freedom? Consider this book a ticket to an unexpected destination—the heart of your being.

Open your wings and prepare for flight!

Spiritual Wisdom on Health and Healing

This booklet is rich with spiritual keys to better health on every level.

Discover the spiritual roots of illness and how gratitude can open your heart to God's love and healing.

Simple spiritual exercises go deep to help you get personal divine guidance and insights.

Revitalize your connection with the true healing power of God's love.

Spiritual Wisdom on Prayer, Meditation, and Contemplation

Bring balance and wonder to your life!

This booklet is a portal to your direct, personal connection with Divine Spirit.

Harold Klemp shows how you can experience the powerful benefits of contemplation—"a conversation with the most secret, most genuine, and most mysterious part of yourself."

Move beyond traditional meditation via dynamic spiritual exercises. Learn about the uplifting chant of HU (an ancient holy name for God), visualization, creative imagination, and other active techniques.

Spiritual Wisdom on Relationships

Find the answers to common questions of the heart, including the truth about soul mates, how to strengthen a marriage, and how to know if a partnership is worth developing.

The spiritual exercises included in this booklet can help you break a pattern of poor relationships and find balance. You'll learn new ways to open your heart to love and enrich your relationship with God.

This booklet is a key for anyone wanting more love to give, more love to get. It's a key to better relationships with everyone in your life.

The Call of Soul

Discover how to find spiritual freedom in this lifetime and the infinite world of God's love for you. Includes a CD with dream and Soul Travel techniques.

Past Lives, Dreams, and Soul Travel

These stories and exercises help you find your true purpose, discover greater love than you've ever known, and learn that spiritual freedom is within reach.

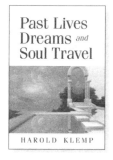

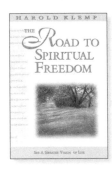

The Road to Spiritual Freedom, Mahanta Transcripts, Book 17

Sri Harold's wisdom and heart-opening stories of everyday people having extraordinary experiences tell of a secret truth at work in *your* life—there is divine purpose and meaning to every experience you have.

How to Survive Spiritually in Our Times, Mahanta Transcripts, Book 16

Discover how to reinvent yourself spiritually—to thrive in a changing world. Stories, tools, techniques, and spiritual insights to apply in your life now.

Autobiography of a Modern Prophet

This riveting story of Harold Klemp's climb up the Mountain of God will help you discover the keys to your own spiritual greatness.

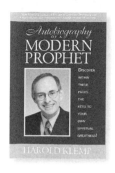

HU, the Most Beautiful Prayer

Singing *HU*, the ancient name for God, can open your heart and lead you to a new understanding of yourself. Includes a CD of the HU song.

Those Wonderful ECK Masters

Would you like to have *personal* experience with spiritual masters that people all over the world—since the beginning of time—have looked to for guidance, protection, and divine love? This book includes real-life stories and spiritual exercises to meet eleven ECK Masters.

The Spiritual Laws of Life

Learn how to keep in tune with your true spiritual nature. Spiritual laws reveal the behind-the-scenes forces at work in your daily life.

GLOSSARY

Words set in SMALL CAPS are defined elsewhere in this glossary.

Blue Light   How the MAHANTA often appears in the inner worlds to the CHELA or seeker.

chela   A spiritual student, often a member of ECKANKAR.

ECK   The Life Force, Holy Spirit, or Audible Life Current which sustains all life.

Eckankar   *EHK-ahn-kahr*   The Path of Spiritual Freedom. Also known as the Ancient Science of SOUL TRAVEL. A truly spiritual way of life for the individual in modern times. The teachings provide a framework for anyone to explore their own spiritual experiences. Established by PAUL TWITCHELL, the modern-day founder, in 1965. The word means Co-worker with God.

ECK Masters   Spiritual Masters who can assist and protect people in their spiritual studies and travels. The ECK Masters are from a long line of God-Realized SOULS who know the responsibility that goes with spiritual freedom.

God-Realization The state of God Consciousness. Complete and conscious awareness of God.

HU *HYOO* The most ancient, secret name for God. It can be sung as a love song to God aloud or silently to oneself to align with God's love.

initiation Earned by a member of ECKANKAR through spiritual unfoldment and service to God. The initiation is a private ceremony in which the individual is linked to the Sound and Light of God.

Karma, Law of The Law of Cause and Effect, action and reaction, justice, retribution, and reward, which applies to the lower or psychic worlds: the Physical, Astral, Causal, Mental, and Etheric PLANES.

Klemp, Harold The present MAHANTA, the LIVING ECK MASTER. SRI Harold Klemp became the Mahanta, the Living ECK Master in 1981. His spiritual name is WAH Z.

Living ECK Master The spiritual leader of ECKANKAR. He leads SOUL back to God. He teaches in the physical world as the Outer Master, in the dream state as the Dream Master, and in the spiritual worlds as the Inner Master. SRI HAROLD KLEMP became the MAHANTA, the Living ECK Master in 1981.

Mahanta An expression of the Spirit of God that is always with you. Sometimes seen as a

BLUE LIGHT or Blue Star or in the form of the
Mahanta, the LIVING ECK MASTER. The highest
state of God Consciousness on earth, only
embodied in the Living ECK Master. He is
the Living Word.

planes   Levels of existence, such as the Physical, Astral, Causal, Mental, Etheric, and SOUL
Planes.

Self-Realization   SOUL recognition. The entering
of Soul into the Soul PLANE and there beholding
Itself as pure Spirit. A state of seeing, knowing, and being.

Shariyat-Ki-Sugmad   The sacred scriptures of
ECKANKAR. The scriptures are comprised of
twelve volumes in the spiritual worlds. The
first two were transcribed from the inner
PLANES by PAUL TWITCHELL, modern-day founder
of Eckankar.

Soul   The True Self, an individual, eternal spark
of God. The inner, most sacred part of each
person. Soul can see, know, and perceive all
things. It is the creative center of Its own world.

Soul Travel   The expansion of consciousness.
The ability of SOUL to transcend the physical
body and travel into the spiritual worlds of
God. Soul Travel is taught only by the LIVING
ECK MASTER. It helps people unfold spiritually
and can provide proof of the existence of God
and life after death.

Sound and Light of ECK   The Holy Spirit. The two aspects through which God appears in the lower worlds. People can experience them by looking and listening within themselves and through SOUL TRAVEL.

Spiritual Exercises of ECK   Daily practices for direct, personal experience with the Sound Current. Creative techniques using contemplation and the singing of sacred words to bring the higher awareness of SOUL into daily life.

Sri   A title of spiritual respect, similar to reverend or pastor, used for those who have attained the Kingdom of God. In ECKANKAR, it is reserved for the MAHANTA, the LIVING ECK MASTER.

Sugmad   *SOOG-mahd*   A sacred name for God. It is the source of all life, neither male nor female, the Ocean of Love and Mercy.

Temples of Golden Wisdom   Golden Wisdom Temples found on the various PLANES—from the Physical to the Anami Lok; CHELAS of ECKANKAR are taken to these temples in the SOUL body to be educated in the divine knowledge; sections of the SHARIYAT-KI-SUGMAD, the sacred teachings of ECK, are kept at these temples.

Twitchell, Paul   An American ECK MASTER who brought the modern teachings of ECKANKAR to

78

the world through his writings and lectures. His spiritual name is Peddar Zaskq.

Wah Z *WAH zee* The spiritual name of Sri Harold Klemp. It means the secret doctrine. It is his name in the spiritual worlds.

For more explanations of Eckankar terms, see *A Cosmic Sea of Words: The ECKANKAR Lexicon,* by Harold Klemp.

ABOUT THE AUTHOR

Award-winning author, teacher, and spiritual guide Sri Harold Klemp helps seekers reach their full potential.

He is the Mahanta, the Living ECK Master and spiritual leader of Eckankar, the Path of Spiritual Freedom. He is the latest in a long line of spiritual Adepts who have served throughout history in every culture of the world.

Sri Harold teaches creative spiritual practices that enable anyone to achieve life mastery and gain inner peace and contentment. His messages are relevant to today's spiritual needs and resonate with every generation.

Sri Harold's body of work includes more than one hundred books, which have been translated into eighteen languages and won multiple awards. The miraculous, true-life stories he shares lift the veil between heaven and earth.

In his groundbreaking memoir, *Autobiography of a Modern Prophet*, he reveals secrets to spiritual success gleaned from his personal journey into the heart of God.

Find your own path to true happiness, wisdom, and love in Sri Harold Klemp's inspired writings.